MINNESOTA

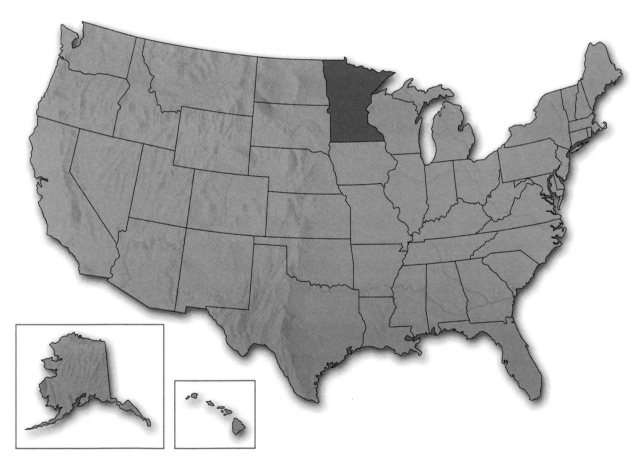

Neil Purslow

Published by Weigl Publishers Inc.
123 South Broad Street, Box 227
Mankato, MN 56002
USA
Web site: http://www.weigl.com

Library of Congress Cataloging-in-Publication Data available upon
request from the publisher. Fax: (507) 388-2746 for the attention of the
Publishing Records Department.

ISBN 1-930954-85-9

Printed in the United States of America
1 2 3 4 5 6 7 8 9 10   05 04 03 02 01

Project Coordinators
Rennay Craats
Michael Lowry
Substantive Editor
Carlotta Lemieux
Copy Editors
Heather Kissock
Jennifer Nault
Designers
Warren Clark
Terry Paulhus
Photo Researcher
Michael Lowry

Photograph Credits

Every reasonable effort has been made to trace ownership and to obtain
permission to reprint copyright material. The publishers would be
pleased to have any errors or omissions brought to their attention so
that they may be corrected in subsequent printings.

Cover: Snoopy (Bob Cole, Mall of America), Lake (Corel Corporation);
© AFP/Corbis/Magma: page 21; ©Alvis Upitis Photography: page 5; Archive Photos:
pages 24 (Victor Malafronte), 29 (Photo File); Bloomington Convention and Visitors
Bureau: page 27; Corel Corporation: pages 7, 9, 10, 11, 13, 14; Corbis Corporation:
pages 14, 15; Eyewire Corporation: page 27; Greyhound Lines: page 5; Mall of
America: page 12; Minnesota Historical Society: pages 6, 7 (Edward Hartman), 16, 17,
17 (Francis Lee Jaques), 18, 19, 20, 29 (John C. Wild); Minnesota Office of Tourism
Photo: pages 3, 4, 6, 7, 8, 9, 10, 11, 12, 13, 15, 20, 22, 23, 24, 25, 26, 27, 28; The
Museum of Questionable Medical Devices: page 24; Reuters/Archive Photos: page 26
(Eric Miller); Saint Paul Convention and Visitors Bureau: page 21; © UFS: page 25;
Walker Art Center: page 20.

CONTENTS

INTRODUCTION

Ninety-seven percent of all children in Minnesota fish its waters.

Minnesota is famous for its many lakes. One of the state's nicknames is "Land of 10,000 Lakes," but there are actually more than 12,000. With so many lakes, fishing and canoeing are popular recreational sports. Minnesota's lakeshores are also home to a variety of cottages, beaches, tourist camps, and resorts.

Because Minnesota is rich in minerals, farmland, and waterways, it has become an important **industrial** state. Food products, machinery and electrical goods, printed materials, medical products, and fabricated metals are all made in Minnesota. The state is part of the Midwestern Corn Belt, where corn crops are raised. Dairy products are also a leading source of income for farmers.

Minneapolis windsurfers need not travel far to enjoy this water sport, the city has twenty-two natural lakes within its limits.

QUICK FACTS

Minnesota has a few different nicknames. It is called the "Gopher State" and the "Bread and Butter State," but it is officially known as the "North Star State."

The state flag has three dates woven into the wreath: 1819, when Fort Snelling was established,1858, when it officially became a state, and 1893, the year the flag was adopted.

The state name comes from a Sioux word meaning "cloudy or sky-colored water." The name refers to the Minnesota River.

On an average day, about 1,400 takeoffs and landings occur at the Minneapolis-Saint Paul International Airport.

Getting There

Minnesota is one of thirteen states that shares a border with Canada. It is also the twelfth largest state. At its widest point Minnesota is 358 miles wide and 406 miles long.

Minnesota is in the north-central United States and is almost right in the middle of North America. Manitoba and Ontario in Canada are its neighbors to the north. North and South Dakota are to the west. Iowa is to the south, and Wisconsin and Lake Superior are to the east.

Most people travel to Minnesota by air or road. A network of highways totaling 130,000 miles criss-crosses the state. The state also boasts more than 365 airports, most of which are private. The largest airport is the Minneapolis-Saint Paul International Airport, which is the nation's tenth busiest.

QUICK FACTS

The highest point in Minnesota is Eagle Mountain at 2,301 feet. It is surrounded by some of the most beautiful parks on the planet. Boundary Water Canoe Wilderness Area and Superior National Forest are natural tourist attractions.

Greyhound Bus Lines began operation in Minnesota in 1914. The first route took miners from Hibbing to several nearby iron mines.

Duluth is the farthest inland water **port** in the nation. The port is 2,300 miles west of the Atlantic Ocean.

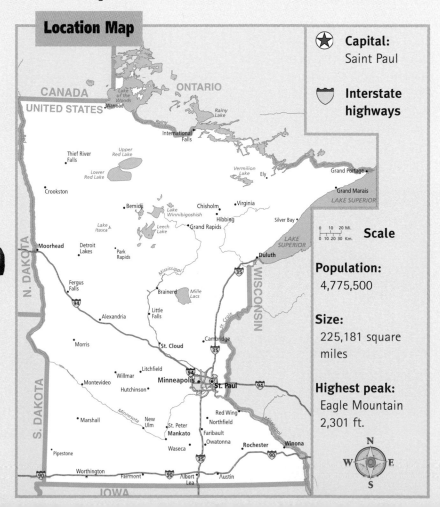

Location Map

Capital: Saint Paul

Interstate highways

Scale
0 10 20 Mi.
0 10 20 30 Km.

Population: 4,775,500

Size: 225,181 square miles

Highest peak: Eagle Mountain 2,301 ft.

Minnesota offers activities for all seasons—from swimming and fishing in summer to skiing and iceboat racing in winter. Many annual festivals attract thousands of local people and visitors from across the country each year.

Minnesota has a number of natural resource industries. Large-scale iron ore mining began in the 1880s. Today, the state continues to be the leading producer of iron ore in the United States. Forestry is also an important industry in Minnesota.

Minneapolis's May Day Parade is full of colorful and imaginative costumes.

QUICK FACTS

Minnesota claims more boats per person than any other state. One person in six owns a boat in Minnesota.

Agate can be found around the Lake Superior area. It is a beautiful quartz stone banded with rich red and orange. These colors come from the iron ore in the soil. Lake Superior agate is Minnesota's official gemstone.

Tobogganing is a great way to enjoy Minnesota's cold winters.

Minnesota maintains 38,000 acres of hardwood forest and woodlands in the southeastern part of the state.

QUICK FACTS

The official state seal shows a barefoot farmer plowing a field near Saint Anthony Falls on the Mississippi River. The farmer's ax, gun, and **powderhorn** rest on a nearby stump as a Native American rides by on a horse.

The blueberry muffin is Minnesota's official state muffin. Wild blueberries are native to northeastern Minnesota and grow in bogs, hillsides, and forested areas.

The common loon, also known as the great northern diver, is the official state bird.

The state capital is Saint Paul, while the state's largest city is Minneapolis.

The pink and white lady slipper is one of the rarest wildflowers. It is illegal to pick this official state flower. The lady slipper thrives in swamps, **bogs**, and damp woods. It grows very slowly and takes from four to sixteen years to produce its first flower. A lady slipper can live up to fifty years and can grow to four feet high.

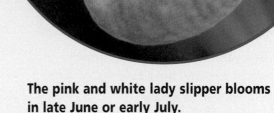

The pink and white lady slipper blooms in late June or early July.

The state fish is the walleye. It lives in all parts of the state but is most numerous in the large, cool lakes of the north. Its eyes are sensitive to light, so it lives in deep, dark water during the day and moves to shallower water at night. Minnesota fishers consider walleye a favorite catch.

Other official state symbols include the morel as the state mushroom, wild rice as the state grain, and milk as the state drink.

The record catch for a walleye in Minnesota is 17 pounds 8 ounces.

Beautiful waterfalls are formed when streams flow over rocky cliffs.

LAND AND CLIMATE

Minnesota is made up of two major natural regions. In the northeastern corner is the Superior Upland, which is part of the Laurentian Upland, or Canadian Shield. This area consists mainly of low, rounded hills of ancient volcanic rock. Many of the basins that were gouged into the rock by **glaciers** have become rock-bottom lakes.

The other area is called the Central Lowland. It covers the largest part of the state. The Central Lowland was sculpted by the last glaciers and is extremely flat. The entire area was once the floor of Lake Agassiz. This lake was created 12,000 years ago when the glacier ice melted. As the lake dried up, it left behind rich soil.

Minnesota's climate tends to be extreme with warm summer temperatures averaging 74 °Fahrenheit and cold winters hovering around 0 °F. The thermometer plunges to –20 °F during cold snaps in winter, making for very chilly days. On the other hand, heat waves are common occurrences in Minnesota summers. Temperatures of 100 °F drive people to the lakes to cool off.

Visitors to the Soudan Underground Mine must wear hard hats as they tour a world beneath the earth.

NATURAL RESOURCES

Minnesota sits on huge reserves of iron ore, a mineral used to make steel. The iron ore is mined from both underground and **open-pit mines**. These mines account for 83 percent of the state's total mineral income. Minnesota is the largest producer of iron ore in the United States.

Long ago, two-thirds of the state was covered with pine forests. Between the late 1800s and the early 1900s, Minnesota was the leading lumber-producing state. After the forests were logged or cleared for farming, production quickly dropped. Today, only one-third of Minnesota is covered in forest. Most of the harvested wood is used to make wood products or to produce pulp and paper.

The Forest History Center contains a recreation of an old logging camp.

QUICK FACTS

The type of iron ore mined in Minnesota is called **taconite**. The ore is shipped to steel mills around the world.

Iron ore mines extend for almost 80 miles along the Mesabi Range in northeastern Minnesota.

Sand, gravel, and stone are other leading mineral products found throughout the state. Lime, clay, peat, and abrasive stone are also mined near Jasper.

Minnesota's timber industry is a big producer of Christmas trees.

PLANTS AND ANIMALS

In the northeast, **coniferous forests** once covered more than one-third of the state. Early logging removed huge amounts of valuable white pine from these forests. Birch, poplar, and other trees have now replaced much of the original forest.

The other two-thirds were mainly **deciduous forest** and tall-grass prairie. In the south, west, and extreme northwest, tall prairie grass once grew everywhere. Because of the deep and fertile soil, these areas have now become farmland.

Minnesota's north is home to black bears, eastern timber wolves, moose, and other large animals. White-tailed deer can be found in every county. Smaller, fur-bearing animals such as raccoons, woodchucks, muskrats, opossums, and skunks also live throughout the state.

QUICK FACTS

Twenty different species of amphibian live in Minnesota, including six species of salamander.

Norway pine is the official state tree. It stands 60 to 100 feet tall with a trunk three to five feet wide. It is also called the red pine because of its reddish-brown bark. The tallest pine is in Itasca Park. It stands 120 feet high and is more than 300 years old.

Five species of tree squirrel live in Minnesota's forested regions, while the gopher prefers to live in more open spaces.

The timber wolf can weigh up to 175 pounds and be as long as 6.5 feet.

Over the years, the number of birds in Minnesota has decreased. The wild turkey, tundra swan, trumpeter swan, sandhill crane, American bald eagle, and peregrine falcon were all in danger of dying out. During the past ten years, these birds have been making a comeback and can now be seen throughout the state.

There are twenty species of amphibian and twenty-nine species of reptile in Minnesota. The American toad, chorus frogs, and tiger salamanders are common residents of the state. The common garter snake is the most numerous snake, while the timber rattlesnake, massasauga rattlesnake, wood turtle, and Blanding's turtle are **endangered** or **threatened**.

QUICK FACTS

Five pairs of peregrine falcons have been nesting in the Minneapolis-Saint Paul area for several years.

There are 153 different species of fish in Minnesota.

Minnesota has twenty fisheries, which contain walleye, trout, salmon, muskellunge, largemouth bass, and sunfish.

The bald eagle is not actually bald, its name comes from the word piebald, meaning "marked with white."

The John Beargrease Sled Dog Marathon is 421 miles long.

QUICK FACTS

More than 42 million people visit the Mall of America each year.

The huge iron ore open-pit mines are very popular tourist attractions.

Superior National Forest covers nearly 3.9 million acres, while the Chippewa National Forest covers 660,000 acres.

TOURISM

Minnesota's lakes, cottages, and hot weather bring tourists from all over the United States. Many come to enjoy the relaxed atmosphere. Others come for the recreational activities. Boating, fishing, and swimming are just a few of the popular summer activities. The Winter Festival in Duluth, the Saint Paul Winter Carnival, and the Grand Portage Chippewa John Beargrease Sled Dog Marathon draw huge crowds during the winter. The marathon is a sled-dog race from Duluth to Grand Portage.

The Mall of America is the largest enclosed retail and entertainment complex in the country. It has more than 400 stores, an 18-hole miniature golf mountain adventure, a 7-acre theme park, a 1.2 million-gallon walk-through aquarium, and a NASCAR Silicon Motor Speedway.

The national parks are always a favorite with campers. One of the largest national forests in the United States is Superior National Forest in the northeast part of the state. Chippewa National Forest is also in Minnesota. It includes Winnibigoshish, Leech, and Cass lakes. As well, Minnesota has 231,000 acres set aside as state parks and forests.

The Mall of America is home to an underwater world where guests can walk through a 400-foot clear tunnel.

Farmers use augers to load crops into storage bins and transport trucks.

INDUSTRY

Agriculture is one of Minnesota's major industries. In the early 1900s, wheat was the state's main agricultural product. Corn and dairy farming have now replaced it. The Midwestern Corn Belt produces corn, oats, and hay. These crops are used to feed large numbers of hogs and cattle. The extra corn is sold within and outside Minnesota.

Manufacturing is another important part of the state's economy. Food processing includes meat packing, dairy products, milling grain, and packaging fruit and vegetables. Iron ore mining, tourism, and forestry continue to be important industries in Minnesota.

QUICK FACTS

Minnesota is one of the leading producers of sugar beets in the United States.

Corn is Minnesota's most important cash crop.

There are more than 3 million people working in Minnesota.

Cropland occupies 42 percent of the state's total land area, with another 3 percent used as pasture.

GOODS AND SERVICES

Minnesota is home to several turbine manufacturers. Turbines make electricity out of water, steam, or gas.

With such a strong agricultural industry, farmers soon formed **cooperatives** to help buy and sell their products. Today, the largest and most important consumer cooperatives are the creameries. Creameries sell milk, butter, cheese, and other dairy products. Other consumer cooperatives sell seed, fertilizers, and machinery to the farmers.

Almost 30 percent of Minnesota's workers have jobs in the service sector. The service sector includes people working in hotels, hospitals, and restaurants. Another 20 percent make their living in the wholesale and retail trade, while 14 percent work in manufacturing.

Some of Minnesota's important goods include industrial machinery, computers, office equipment, refrigeration and service machinery, and electronic and electrical equipment. Printing and publishing are busy industries throughout the state.

Milk from creameries was once delivered in glass bottles and was transported in wire carriers.

QUICK FACTS

The Twin Cities is the phrase often used to describe the Minneapolis-Saint Paul **metropolitan** area.

Sugar refining is largely centered in the Red River Valley. That is where the sugar beets are grown.

Minnesota ranks fifth in the nation in the sale of milk and dairy products.

One of the United States' largest plants for processing and packaging Chinese food is in Duluth.

Barges have no engines, so they require another boat to push or pull them.

Barges haul grain, coal, petroleum products, and other big loads up the Mississippi River as far north as Minneapolis. Barge traffic, however, is being replaced by other forms of transportation, such as trains. There are more than 4,500 miles of railroad track in use in Minnesota.

Minneapolis was once a major center for **flour milling** and grain processing. Most of the nation's leading flour-milling companies still have their head offices in Minneapolis, even though little of the milling is done there now.

Years ago, Minnesota used water power to produce electricity. As industries grew, the need for power became too great for these plants. Today, 70 percent of Minnesota's power comes from plants that burn coal, crude oil, and natural gas. Only 2 percent is produced with hydropower, and the rest comes from three nuclear power plants.

QUICK FACTS

Coal is the main source of fuel burned in power plants to create electricity.

Minneapolis used to be known as the Mill City.

The Post-it® note was developed by the 3M Company, whose head office is in Saint Paul.

Trains are one of the most efficient ways to carry bulk cargo over long distances.

The Ojibwe people are also known by the names Anishinabe and Chippewa.

FIRST NATIONS

Native Americans were the first people to live in Minnesota, possibly as long as 8000 years ago. Early groups built piles of earth in different sizes and shapes, each one used for a different purpose. It was because of this practice that these early peoples became known as the Mound Builders. Some mounds were used as bases for public buildings, houses of leaders, and temples. Other mounds were used as funeral monuments and burial chambers.

In the late seventeenth century, the Ojibwe people **migrated** west into Minnesota as settlers moved in from the east. Many of the Mound Builders then moved to the buffalo ranges of the Great Plains in the Dakotas. Warfare with the Ojibwe forced the Mound Builders to move.

Ojibwe homes were built on pole frames called wigwams.

Native Americans often aided the early European explorers.

The Mound Builders, who later moved west, became known as the Dakotas or, as the settlers called them, the Sioux. The Ojibwe who remained in central Minnesota supported themselves by hunting deer, bear, moose, waterfowl, and small game. They also fished, gathered wild rice, maple sugar, and berries and grew crops.

By the end of the nineteenth century, the number of Ojibwe had fallen to a few hundred. They lived on the Mille Lacs Reservation. Since then, they have rebuilt the reservation, strengthened its traditions, and found new ways to make money and become independent.

The Mille Lacs Reservation occupies 61,000 acres of land around the southern end of Mille Lacs Lake.

QUICK FACTS

Birchbark sheets were used for keeping records of tribal affairs.

Ojibwe covered their homes with birchbark or woven reed mats.

Fur traders are an important part of Minnesota's history.

Great Britain lost its claim to the area of Minnesota east of the Mississippi River to the United States, in 1783. Then in 1803, the United States acquired the area west of the Mississippi River from France.

The Sieur de La Vérendrye was the last of the major French explorers. He explored the northern Great Plains region of the United States.

The city of Duluth was named for the French explorer Daniel Greysolon Du Luth.

Jesuit missionaries Michel Guignas and Nicholas de Gonner built the first church in Minnesota.

EXPLORERS AND MISSIONARIES

French fur traders Pierre Esprit Radisson and Médard Chouart des Groseilliers were the first Europeans to visit the Minnesota area in 1660. They were looking for furs in the Great Lakes region. In 1680, Daniel Greysolon Du Luth entered Minnesota by way of Lake Superior and the Saint Louis River. He claimed much of Minnesota for France.

Father Louis Hennepin was a French priest sent to explore the upper Mississippi River. In 1680, he discovered and named the Falls of Saint Anthony, which later became the site of the Twin Cities. Soon after, the French began trading furs along the Mississippi and Minnesota rivers.

Fur trader René Boucher traveled to Minnesota in 1727. His expedition eventually arrived on the shore of Lake Pepin. A fort was built on the site and became known as Fort Beauharnois.

Some of the early French explorers were looking for a river that would take them to the Pacific Ocean. They hoped the Mississippi River would do so.

Settlers took over lands which once belonged to Native Americans.

EARLY SETTLERS

Between 1849 and 1863, several treaties were signed with the Native American peoples. These treaties turned over most of the Native American land to the United States. Settlers then flocked to the Mississippi and Minnesota River valleys to farm the fertile soil.

In 1857, Henry M. Rice won a federal land grant to build a railroad in Minnesota. The state railroad was designed to have Saint Paul and Minneapolis as the key trading centers.

By 1883, the national transcontinental railway was finished. It connected the Twin Cities to the Pacific Ocean and the eastern flour markets. The Twin Cities soon became a major center for lumber heading west to the treeless plains and for returning shipments of wheat.

Fueled by the growth of farming, lumbering, and iron mining, the state's population increased tremendously in the thirty-five years after the Civil War. With the exception of a few northern areas, Minnesota was settled by 1900.

QUICK FACTS

Between 1853 and 1857, the number of Minnesotan settlers grew from 40,000 to 150,000 .

Minnesota experienced three great crises during its first seven years of statehood: a depression, the American Civil War, and a war with the Dakota.

During another huge growth spurt from 1865 to 1900, Minnesota's population grew from 250,000 to over 1,750,000.

Alexander Ramsey was the first territorial governor of Minnesota.

The transcontinental railway was built by two companies, the Union Pacific and the Southern Pacific.

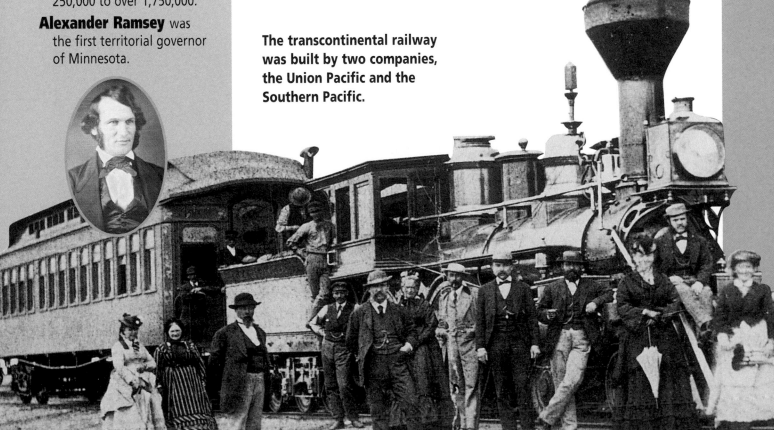

Minneapolis is the largest city in Minnesota and one of the largest cities in the upper Midwest.

POPULATION

More than 70 percent of Minnesota's population lives in towns or cities. The total population of the state in 1999 was 4,775,500 people.

The population of central Minneapolis is dropping as families move to the suburbs and the land is taken up by businesses. The city of Saint Paul continues to grow, but at a very slow rate. However, the total **metropolitan** area of the Twin Cities and their suburbs is growing rapidly.

About 93 percent of Minnesota's population is made up of people of European descent. Another 3 percent are African American, 2.6 percent Asians and Pacific Islanders, and 1.2 percent Native Americans. Most of the Native Americans in Minnesota are Ojibwe or Sioux. The Ojibwe live in the Twin Cities area or on reservations in the north. The Sioux live mainly in the southern counties.

QUICK FACTS

Half of Minnesota's inhabitants live in the Twin Cities metropolitan area.

Duluth, the port city on Lake Superior, is 26 miles long and less than a mile wide as it hugs the lake's shoreline.

Minnehaha Falls lies within the city limits of Minneapolis. The falls were made famous by Henry Wadsworth Longfellow's poem "Song of Hiawatha."

The Minnesota State Fair is held once a year in Saint Paul. The fair lasts for a week and attracts more than 1.6 million visitors.

POLITICS AND GOVERNMENT

Minnesota was made a territory in 1849 and became the thirty-second state of the Union in 1858. When Minnesota was a territory, the government was dominated by the Democratic Party. With the formation of the Republican Party in 1855, Democratic power decreased.

In 1857, a convention was held to draw up a constitution for the state. The Democratic and Republican parties were so divided over slavery that they met separately and drafted separate constitutions. After five weeks of talking, they reached an agreement. Voters approved the new constitution in that year's election.

Today twelve percent of Minnesota's labor force works for federal, state, or local government. The state legislature consists of two houses. The House of Representatives has 134 members, and the Senate has 67 members. The legislature meets for 120 days over a two-year period. It decides such matters as taxation, welfare programs, crime, and education.

The city of Saint Paul was given its name in 1841 by the French priest Reverend Lucien Galtier. Galtier chose the name in honor of his favorite saint.

Minnesota's State Capitol is located in downtown Saint Paul.

QUICK FACTS

In 1999, Jesse Ventura was elected to a four-year term as governor of Minnesota. Before that he was a professional wrestler.

The state sends two senators and eight representatives to Federal Congress.

The Heritagefest in New Ulm is a celebration of German culture.

CULTURAL GROUPS

The rich farmlands and forests of Minnesota attracted settlers from all over the world. French Canadians, Swedes, Norwegians, Danes, Germans, and Irish were some of Minnesota's first settlers. They were soon joined by immigrants from Finland, Poland, modern day Czech Republic, and Slovakia.

Today, Minnesotans of German origin form the largest ethnic group. A number of different ethnic festivals are held throughout the state each year. Ethnic Days in Chisholm celebrates the cultural groups in the northeastern part of Minnesota. In September, a public powwow by the Dakota people at Mankato celebrates their traditional ways.

QUICK FACTS

The Logging Days festival in Bemidji includes horse-drawn teams, traditional equipment, lumberjack pancakes, and throwing contests.

The annual Western Minnesota Steam Threshers Reunion is held in Rollag. It is an exhibition of steam-powered farm machinery from the past. This equipment helped make the farming industry what it is today.

The Scottish Country Fair is held each year at Macalester College. This Celtic festival has one of the nation's best Highland Games.

Every October the town of Albert Lea plays host to the Big Islands Rendezvous, a showcase of early fur trading life.

QUICK FACTS

The Mille Lacs Reservation now enjoys many new facilities, including a new community center and a new ceremonial center.

Snowshoes were invented by Native Americans who lived in the Great Lakes region. Snowshoes distribute a person's weight across a larger surface area, preventing them from sinking in the snow.

In 1988, the Gaming Regulatory Act recognized Native Americans' right to own and operate casino and gaming businesses on reservation lands. By the early 1990s, the Ojibwe had opened the Grand Casino Mille Lacs and Grand Casino Hinckley on the reservation. The Ojibwe used the money from the casinos to rejuvenate their culture and reservation, as well as to benefit the entire region. The annual powwow in Hinckley attracts Native Americans from all over the Midwest. They perform traditional, fancy, jingle, and grass dancing.

The Hinckley powwow holds numerous competitive singing and dancing contests.

Participants in a powwow use dance, costume, and song to tell a story.

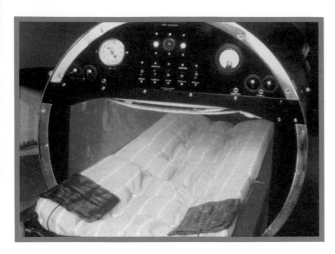

The inventor of the MacGregor Rejuvenator claimed that it could reverse the ageing process.

Famous actors who were born in Minnesota are Judy Garland, Jane Russell, Jessica Lange, E.G. Marshall, and Winona Ryder.

The Science Museum of Minnesota in Saint Paul provides a unique mix of natural history, environmental science, biology, physics, and high-tech fun.

Jean Paul Getty was one of the richest men in the world. He was born in Minneapolis.

ARTS AND ENTERTAINMENT

There are some strange and fascinating museums in Minnesota. The Museum of Questionable Medical Devices, located in Minneapolis, explores the collection of **quack** medical devices found in the United States. Visitors can sample the devices, and even get a **phrenology** reading by having the lumps on their heads measured. The lumps are believed by some to be related to a person's personality and intelligence. The devices on display at the museum are examples of how some people have tried to analyze and cure themselves and others using non-scientific methods.

Saint Paul is home to the well-known Minnesota Children's Museum. Here children can burrow through a giant anthill, go on stage in a TV or music studio, create a thunderstorm, and operate a big crane. This is the place where children can get hands-on experience by touching, climbing, splashing, crawling, pushing, and pulling.

Visitors to the Minnesota Children's Museum can explore Earth World. Earth World introduces children to the secrets of the natural world.

The *Spoonbridge and Cherry* is one of the more than forty works of art that can be found at the Sculpture Garden in Minneapolis.

There are several art galleries in Minnesota. Some of the more popular are the Walker Art Center, the American Swedish Institute, the Sculpture Garden, and the Minneapolis Institute of Arts. These galleries show art ranging from historical to modern and from local to international.

Tyrone Guthrie, an English stage director and actor, helped establish the Minnesota Theater Company in 1963. The Guthrie Theater is named after him. There are many other theaters in the state to entertain Minnesotans.

The Minnesota Orchestra is one of the great symphony orchestras in the United States. It makes its home in Orchestra Hall in downtown Minneapolis. The hall is famous for the acoustic cubes on its ceiling and stage walls. These cubes deflect the sound so that the audience can hear the performance perfectly.

QUICK FACTS

Musician Bob Dylan was also born in Minnesota.

The Minneapolis Symphony Orchestra was founded in 1903. In 1968 the name was changed to the Minnesota Orchestra.

Charles Schulz, the creator of the *Charlie Brown* comic strip, was born in Minneapolis.

The Walker Art Museum is home to over 8,000 pieces of art.

The Metrodome in Minneapolis is home to both the Minnesota Twins and the Minnesota Vikings.

SPORTS

Minnesota is the place to be for professional sports. The Twin Cities boast seven different professional sports teams in six different sports. The Minnesota Vikings play in the National Football League, while the Minnesota Twins compete in Major League Baseball. There are currently two professional basketball teams—the Timberwolves in the NBA and the Lynx in the WNBA. The Minnesota Thunder leads the way for professional soccer as does the Minnesota Blue Ox for roller hockey. Professional ice hockey made a return to the state with the introduction of the Minnesota Wild in the 2000–2001 season.

Whether they are catching trophy-sized pike in the cold northern waters, fly-fishing on the southern streams, or wrestling lake trout on Lake Superior, Minnesotan's never run out of places to fish. The many bodies of water offer other activities as well, such as water skiing, yachting, kayaking, canoeing, motorboating, and inner-tubing on the Red Lake River.

QUICK FACTS

Roger Maris held the home run title for nearly thirty-seven years. He was born in Hibbing, Minnesota.

Minnesota has hundreds of miles of hiking trails, many of which wind along the lakes and rivers.

Cyclists enjoy 250 miles of paved trails built along old railroad beds. Minnesota has more paved rail-to-trail bikeways than any other state in the country.

Golf is a popular pastime in Minnesota with over 450 golf courses in the state.

The Minnesota Vikings uniform colors are purple, gold, and white.

Ski areas around the Twin Cities use floodlights for night skiing.

Outdoor sports are not limited to the summer. Popular winter sports in Minnesota include skiing, snowboarding, snowmobiling, snowshoeing, and dog sledding. Minnesota is the envy of the nation when it comes to cross-country ski and snowmobile trails. It is also home to the largest and highest downhill ski area in the Midwest.

High schools, colleges, and universities throughout the state have very active sports programs. Students in these programs compete in all kinds of events throughout the year. Scholarships are offered to athletes who attend and compete in college and university sports.

QUICK FACTS

Rushing Rapids Parkway is where the St. Louis River thunders through a rocky gorge and over slabs of ancient rock. White water rafting is the only way you can get through these rapids.

Water skiing was invented on Lake Pepin, the widest point of the Mississippi River.

White water rafting is a thrilling way to explore Minnesota's great outdoors.

Brain Teasers

1

Does wild rice grow naturally in Minnesota?

Answer: Yes. For many years, all of the wild rice in the world came from Minnesota. It grows in the shallow waters of the lakes in central and northern Minnesota.

2

The state bird is the common loon. How many loons make their home in Minnesota each year?

Answer: 12,000

3

The lowest elevation point in Minnesota is on the shore of Lake Superior and is:

a. 0 feet (sea level)

b. 327 feet

c. 602 feet

d. 1,028 feet

Answer: c. 602 feet

4

TRUE OR FALSE?

Minnesota produces 9.7 billion pounds of milk per year.

Answer: True. Minnesota is ranked fifth in the nation for milk production.

5 Roger Maris was born in Minnesota and held the major league baseball home run crown from 1961 until 1998. How many home runs did he hit?

Answer: Sixty-one

6 At one time Minnesota was completely covered by a glacier. About how many years ago did this happen?

a. 50,000 years ago

b. 14,000 years ago

c. 12,000 years ago

d. 9,900 years ago

Answer: b. 14,000 years ago

7 The many libraries and museums in the Twin Cities make the area a cultural center for the Midwest. How many libraries are there?

Answer: 130

8 MAKE A GUESS!

The first schools in Minnesota were taught by the wives of the officers who worked in the forts. Which of the forts had the first recorded school in Minnesota?

Answer: Fort Snelling

FOR MORE INFORMATION

Books

Breining, Greg. *Minnesota*. Compass American Guide Series. Oakland, CA: Compass American Guides, 1997.

Marsh, Carole. *Christopher Columbus comes to Minnesota!* Carole Marsh Minnesota Books. Peachtree City, GA: Gallopade Publishing Group, 1991.

Weinberger, Mark. *Short Bike Rides in Minnesota: Rides for the Casual Cyclist.* Guilford, CT: Globe Pequot Press, 1998.

Marsh, Carole. *Minnesota Festival!* Carole Marsh Minnesota Books. Peachtree City, GA: Gallopade Publishing Group, 1991.

Web sites

You can also go online and have a look at the following Web sites:

Explore Minnesota
http://www.exploreminnesota.com

Minnesota Historical Society
http://www.mnhs.org

Minnesota Tourism
http://www.minnesotatourism.com

50 States: Minnesota
http://www.50states.com/minnesot.htm

Minnesota Children's Museum
http://www.mcm.org

Some Web sites stay current longer than others. To find other Minnesota Web sites, enter search terms such as "Minnesota," "Mall of America," "Charles Schulz," or any other topic you want to research.

GLOSSARY

barges: long, flat-bottomed boats used for carrying cargo on rivers

bogs: wet, spongy ground

coniferous forests: forests where the trees keep their leaves in winter, for example: pine, cedar, spruce, fir

cooperatives: businesses owned by their members with profits shared between them

deciduous forest: a forest where the trees lose their leaves every year, for example: maple, oak, elm

endangered: plants or animals at risk of becoming extinct

flour milling: grinding and sifting wheat, rye, and other grains into flour for making bread and cakes

glaciers: large, slow moving rivers of ice

industrial: having to do with or produced by industry, for example: iron smelting, coal mining, making plastics

metropolitan: the area surrounding and including a large city

migrated: to have moved from one place to another

open-pit mines: huge holes in the ground where minerals are loaded into trucks and hauled away for processing

phrenology: the idea that a person's personality can be discovered by reading the bumps on their head with a machine

port: a harbor where goods are imported and exported

powderhorn: an animal horn used to load gunpowder into muskets

precipitation: rain or snow falling to the ground

quack: something that is a fraud or a scam

taconite: a flint-like rock that contains low-grade iron ore

threatened: plants or animals at risk of becoming endangered

INDEX